MOON
LANDING

THE RACE FOR THE MOON

Yuri Gagarin travelled into space in the Vostok 1 capsule.

The Apollo 11 astronauts travelled into Earth's atmosphere on their way home.

The Apollo 11 crew were Neil Armstrong, Michael Collins, and Edwin Aldrin.

Neil Armstrong and Edwin Aldrin moved into *Eagle* ready to land on the Moon.

Astronauts trained for the weightless conditions of space.

The lunar module *Eagle* on the Moon's surface

MOON LANDING

THE RACE FOR THE MOON

Written by
CAROLE STOTT

Illustrated by
RICHARD BONSON

DK

DORLING KINDERSLEY
LONDON • NEW YORK • MOSCOW • SYDNEY
www.dk.com

A DORLING KINDERSLEY BOOK
www.dk.com

Senior Editor Scarlett O'Hara
Senior Art Editor Vicky Wharton
Senior Managing Editor Linda Martin
Senior Managing Art Editor Julia Harris
DTP Designer Andrew O'Brien
Picture Researcher Amanda Russell
Jacket Designer Andrew Nash
Production Kate Oliver

First published in 1999
by Dorling Kindersley Limited,
9 Henrietta Street, Covent Garden,
London WC2E 8PS

2 4 6 8 10 9 7 5 3 1

A CIP catalogue record for this book is available
from the British Library.

ISBN 0 7513 5886 X

Reproduced by Colourscan, Singapore
Printed and bound by L.E.G.O., Italy

Additional illustrations by Andrew Wheatcroft and
David Ashby

For Ellen, Owen, Louise, and Alexandra, the
next generation of Moon explorers, from CS.

Contents

Looking into Space

This illustration, drawn by Méliès in 1902, was produced for a film called *Voyage to the Moon*.

FOR THOUSANDS OF YEARS, PEOPLE ON Earth have looked into space and seen the Moon. Its bright, full disc lit up the dark night hours for early people, and inspired countless myths and stories. Its changing face and movement across the sky marked the passage of time. The Moon has always been a fascinating place that some people dreamed of visiting. About a hundred years ago, these dreams started to come true.

Dark areas indicate lower, flatter regions where a spacecraft could land.

Large bowl-shaped hollows, called craters, can be seen from Earth.

FIRST ATTEMPTS

These 17th-century soldiers could shoot all the arrows from a basket at the same time.

Rocket power
Rockets were first used about a thousand years ago by Chinese people, not for travel but as weapons. When the gunpowder inside the rocket was lit, the rocket thrust forward towards the enemy.

EARLY PEOPLE DREAMED OF BEING carried to the Moon by birds or balloons. Realistic ideas of space travel were only developed at the end of the 19th century. The pioneers of space exploration knew that sending anything or anyone into space required a form of transport powerful enough to get away from the pull of Earth's gravity.

They first designed, and later built, a space rocket to do this job. The successful launch of a rocket was followed by the first cargo to be carried into space, the satellite Sputnik, and then by the first living passenger, a dog called Laika. The launch of the first human into space was getting closer.

FACT file

● Goddard's first liquid-fuel rocket was launched on 16 March 1926. It surged upwards for two and a half seconds and reached a height of 12.5 m (41 ft).

● Once the V2 reached a speed of 5,800 kph (3,600 mph) its engine cut out and its 9,988-kg (2,200-lb) bomb coasted for about 96.5 km (60 miles).

● Sputnik 1 was an aluminium sphere 58 cm (22.75 in) in diameter. It was launched on 4 October 1957 and signalled "bleep-bleep" for 21 days.

PROBLEM SOLVING
One man who dreamed of going into space was a Soviet teacher named Konstantin Tsiolkovsky. He worked through the problems of getting a rocket into space, calculating how fast it should go and how much fuel it needed to pull away from Earth's gravity.

FIRST ROCKET
Robert Goddard, an American, not only designed rockets to travel into space but built them, too. He launched the first rocket using liquid fuel in 1926. Its short but successful flight encouraged Goddard and other rocket scientists to continue designing and building. It was not long before a rocket powerful enough to escape Earth's gravity was ready for liftoff.

Tsiolkovsky didn't build the rockets he designed. This model shows what one of his rockets would look like. Space travellers lived above the fuel and engines.

Robert Goddard holds the frame support of his liquid fuel rocket before takeoff in 1926.

	C.2000 BC	C.500 BC	C.270 BC	1609

The Moon through time
The Moon has always interested humans and influenced their lives. It has been worshipped and studied by many cultures.

STONEHENGE
Ancient people watched the Moon. They saw it go through a cycle of phases every 29.5 days and used this as a basis for a calendar.

MOON GODDESS
Early people in countries as far apart as Japan, Italy, and Mexico worshipped Moon goddesses and believed the Moon regulated life and fertility.

HOW FAR?
Scientific study of the Moon began thousands of years ago. Aristarchos calculated the distance between Earth and the Moon around 270 BC.

TELESCOPIC VIEW
Thomas Harriot used the newly invented telescope to study the Moon in July 1609. He, and others, saw mountains and craters on its surface.

Once in space, the four antennas folded out.

Sputnik 1 contained a battery and a radio transmitter, as well as instruments to measure conditions in space such as temperature.

> "A satellite...will be the first step in solving the problem of space flight and will enable our scientists to probe more deeply into the secrets of the universe."
>
> USSR Space Council, 1953

The V2 became the first mass-produced, long-range rocket.

FIRST SATELLITE

Once a rocket for space travel had been developed, scientists worked on their second aim, to put an object into orbit around Earth. The Soviets achieved this in 1957 when the first man-made satellite orbited our planet. As Sputnik 1 circled Earth every 96 minutes, it sent out a bleep-bleep signal.

In the 1940s, the V2 was the largest rocket bomb ever constructed.

During World War II, more than 4,000 V2s were launched against Great Britain.

The satellite carrying Laika was launched from the USSR on 3 November 1957.

SPACE TRAVELLER

No one was sure what effect rocket travel or space itself would have on humans. Animals such as mice, squirrel monkeys, and chimpanzees were the first passengers to try out rocket travel. The first living creature to travel into space was a mongrel dog called Laika. She was launched aboard Sputnik 2 in November 1957. She survived for a week and died when her air was used up.

Air, food, and water in the cabin kept Laika alive for a week in space.

Laika's space capsule was padded to protect her.

Equipment to monitor Laika's heart and breathing was attached to her body so that scientists on the ground would know how she was coping.

POWERFUL WEAPON

A team of rocket engineers working in Germany built a powerful rocket called the V2. They launched it for the first time in 1942 and used it as a rocket bomb in World War II. After the war, the head of the German team, Wernher von Braun, worked in the US to develop rockets for space travel.

MID 1700S	1840	LATE 1800S	1920S	1957
MOON MAPPING Astronomers studied the Moon with more powerful telescopes. They named the features they saw and made maps of the Moon's surface.	**ON CAMERA** When the camera was invented, the Moon was one of the first objects to be photographed. It was first photographed in 1840.	**SPACE FICTION** The author Jules Verne wrote about space travel. His stories combined fact with fiction – in one tale travellers landed on the Moon.	**ROCKET SCIENCE** Space enthusiasts in Europe and America started to build rockets for space. The Moon, the closest object to Earth, became a target for space travel.	**SPACE AGE** Sputnik 1 marked the start of the Space Age. The US and USSR were the first countries to launch rockets into space.

Yuri Gagarin
Gagarin was 27 when he made his historic flight into space. He trained to be a metal worker but had learned to fly in his spare time so that he could join the Soviet Air Force. He became a test pilot, flying new and experimental aircraft. In 1960, Gagarin joined a small team of cosmonauts (Soviet astronauts) training for space. Less than a year later, he was chosen to make the first manned flight.

Gagarin's rocket

GAGARIN'S ROCKET was a Vostok A1. It launched him into space in three stages and had completed its work within minutes.

Nose cone

Vostok capsule

Orbital, third stage

Central rocket, second stage

Booster rockets, first stage

Gagarin's round cabin

Instrument module

Vostok 1 capsule
Gagarin travelled in the Vostok 1 capsule at the top of the rocket. The capsule had a cabin and an instrument module.

Vostok A1 launcher
The first stage lifted the rocket off the launch pad, the second boosted the craft into space, and the third placed the spacecraft in orbit. All three stages and the nose cone were discarded once their work was finished.

THE FIRST MAN IN SPACE

IN EARLY 1961, SPACE SCIENTISTS IN the US and the USSR were working towards launching a human into space. Many people believed that the first flight might be just weeks, or at the most, months away. But when, on 12 April 1961, television stations and newspapers proclaimed, "Gagarin: First Man in Space", almost everyone was taken by surprise. There had been no launch party or live television coverage of the event, and few people knew that there was to be a flight that day. Now Yuri Gagarin was a hero, and his achievement was talked about around the world.

The retrorocket fired to prepare for re-entry to Earth's atmosphere.

The instrument module housed equipment for guiding and controlling the craft in orbit, as well as its braking systems.

Gagarin's flight lasted one orbit of Earth, giving him plenty of time to experience weightlessness.

During his flight, Gagarin constantly answered questions and carried out assignments.

Vostok's orbit

Engels

Baikonur Cosmodrome

Caspian Sea

Aral Sea

IN ORBIT
Vostok 1 travelled at about 28,000 kph (17,400 mph) and orbited Earth at between 181 and 327 km (112 and 203 miles) above the ground.

THE BEGINNING
The Vostok A1 rocket started its journey into space at 9:07 a.m. Moscow time, on 12 April 1961. It set off from the Baikonur Cosmodrome, east of the Aral Sea in the Soviet Union. Gagarin's wife Valya saw him off.

TAKEOFF
Gagarin heard a roar, and the rocket quivered as it left the launch pad. As he moved away from the ground, gravity pulled him down into his seat.

SAFE LANDING

The dangerous part of the flight for Gagarin was the return to Earth. As he passed over Africa, the retrorockets fired, and Vostok 1 slowed down and came out of orbit. Gagarin's craft would land automatically, but he was ready to pilot it himself if necessary. As he left space, gravity pushed him into his seat, and he prepared to be ejected.

The instrument module separated from the cabin before the return to Earth.

ALL GOING WELL
Gagarin sucked water from a tube and found that drops floated about the cabin. The flight had no ill effects on Gagarin. Both his heartbeat and breathing were normal.

Gagarin's small parachute opened first.

7 km (4.3 miles) above the ground the capsule hatch blew off and Gagarin was ejected in his seat.

At 4 km (2.5 miles) above the ground the main parachute opened, and the ejector seat fell to Earth.

Gagarin and Vostok 1 landed in fields 26 km (16 miles) south west of Engels.

The complete capsule was 2.4 m (7.9 ft) in diameter.

A camera in the cabin recorded Gagarin's movements.

ON THE GROUND
Gagarin returned to Earth by a separate parachute from Vostok 1. His main parachute slowed his fall so that he moved at about 5 m (16 ft) per second when he reached the ground.

During the flight, Gagarin recorded his experiences with a pencil in a log book; when he let them go, they floated in the weightlessness of space.

AROUND THE WORLD

Gagarin's space journey took him once around the Earth. He travelled eastwards, moving over his own country from the launch site, then over South America and Africa. From launch to landing, the journey lasted 108 minutes. While in flight, he achieved many firsts: as well as being the first person in space, he was also the first person to talk to Earth from space, and the first person to eat in space.

Returning to Earth

The capsule showed the scars of its return from space. As it travelled through the atmosphere, the outside of the capsule became intensely hot. Gagarin noticed a red glow outside, but inside the temperature didn't rise. The capsule's heat-resistant cover successfully protected him.

VOSTOK 1'S LANDING
The capsule returned to Earth by parachute. This landing would have been too harsh for a cosmonaut inside.

The return to Earth was at 10:55 a.m. Moscow time, 108 minutes after launch.

COSMONAUT TRAINER
Gagarin became the head of cosmonaut training, but he never returned to space. He was killed test-flying a plane in 1968.

> "Weightlessness does not feel unpleasant. Am feeling fine. All instruments and all systems are functioning well."
>
> Yuri Gagarin during his spaceflight, 12 April 1961

A world hero

Everyone wanted to meet the man who had been into space. Gagarin visited countries around the world, including England (above). Wherever he went crowds gathered. He was met by world leaders, given honours and medals, and his home town of Gzhatsk was renamed Gagarin.

Target: the Moon

THE FIRST MAN IN SPACE, YURI GAGARIN, BLASTED OFF in April 1961. Other astronauts got their chance in the months and years to come. The space travellers came from the Soviet Union and the United States. At first they went singly, then in crews of two or three. They stayed in the space close to Earth. But longer missions were being planned. Future trips would take humans to another world – the Moon.

In 1965, Ed White became the first US astronaut to leave his craft and walk in space.

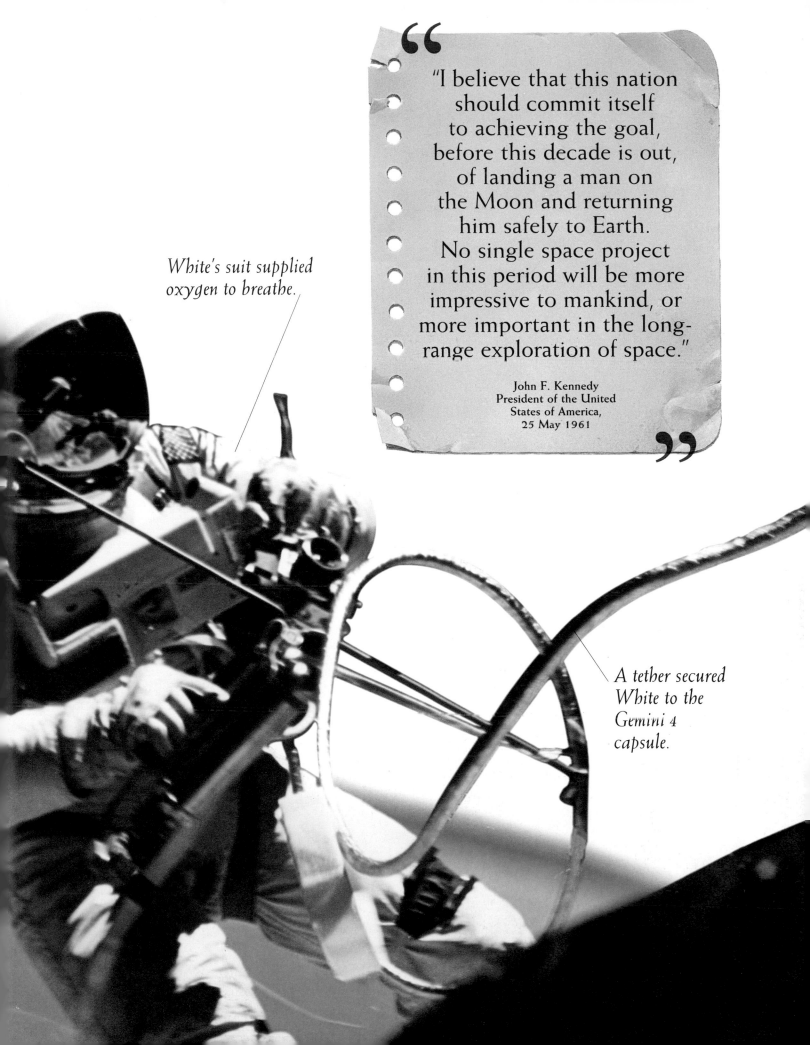

White's suit supplied oxygen to breathe.

"I believe that this nation should commit itself to achieving the goal, before this decade is out, of landing a man on the Moon and returning him safely to Earth. No single space project in this period will be more impressive to mankind, or more important in the long-range exploration of space."

John F. Kennedy
President of the United
States of America,
25 May 1961

A tether secured White to the Gemini 4 capsule.

THE SPACE RACE

GAGARIN'S SUCCESSFUL SPACE FLIGHT IN April 1961 surprised the US. They reacted by declaring that they would send a man to the Moon by the end of the 1960s. Perhaps the Soviets were also aiming to land a man on the Moon; no one was sure. But the two nations began an unofficial race. They both wanted to be the first to make significant steps in space travel. The Soviets launched the first woman into space, made the first spacewalk, and landed the first craft on the Moon. The Americans flew the Mercury and Gemini missions putting crews of two and then three men in space, achieved the first meeting of two craft in space, and made the first space docking. The US slowly gained the lead in the space race and moved closer to its goal.

A DAY IN SPACE

Cosmonaut Gherman Titov was the second Soviet in space. His flight aboard Vostok 2 in August 1961 was four months after Yuri Gagarin's. Titov was the first to spend more than a day in space; his flight lasted a little over 25 hours.

AMERICAN HERO

John Glenn (left) was the first American to orbit Earth. His Mercury 6 capsule, named *Friendship 7*, carried him round Earth three times on 20 February 1962. Back home he was greeted by US President John F. Kennedy.

THE MERCURY 7

The first astronauts from the US travelled into space in bell-shaped capsules, only 2.7 m (9 ft) long. The seven astronauts, chosen in 1959, were known as the Mercury 7. All flights made by the astronauts, between July 1961 and May 1963, were successful. America's second space programme called Gemini began in 1964. Gemini missions carried two men and stayed in space longer.

Alan Shepard

Virgil Grissom

Gordon Cooper

Donald Slayton

John Glenn

Walter Schirra

Scott Carpenter

FIRST WOMAN
Soviet cosmonaut Valentina Tereshkova was the first woman to go into space. She was chosen from a group of five women who trained for the flight. Her capsule Vostok 6 orbited the Earth for three days in June 1963. Her flight took her within 4.8 km (3 miles) of another cosmonaut who spent five days inside Vostok 5.

SPACEWALK
The first astronaut to go outside a craft in space was the Soviet cosmonaut Alexei Leonov in March 1965. His extra vehicular activity (EVA), more usually called a spacewalk, lasted a little longer than expected. His suit had expanded when he was outside the craft, and it was a tight squeeze to get back in through the hatch.

Leonov tumbled about in space for 12 minutes.

A camera was attached to the edge of the airlock.

Leonov moved from the capsule through an airlock into space.

A porthole with a sighting device

Pavel Belyayev, Leonov's fellow cosmonaut, remained inside Voskhod 2.

Nitrogen and oxygen fuel tanks

A communication antenna unfolded once the capsule was in space.

This photograph was taken by the astronauts on board Gemini 6 as they approached Gemini 7 in space.

SPACE RENDEZVOUS
Gemini craft achieved the first rendezvous, or meeting, in space in December 1965. It was an essential manoeuvre for a mission to the Moon. Gemini 7 was already in space when Gemini 6 was launched. To achieve the rendezvous, Gemini 6 flew within 60 cm (2 ft) of Gemini 7.

Gemini 7

Circular rendezvous-antenna in the nose

DOCKING IN SPACE
The next stage after attaining a space rendezvous was for two craft to dock (to meet and then join together) in space. The US gained another space first, when Gemini 8 docked with an uncrewed Agena rocket (above) in March 1966. Gemini 8 was guided by astronaut Neil Armstrong.

The Luna programme
A series of space probes called Luna accomplished many "firsts" for the Soviets. Luna 3 was the first craft to travel around the Moon. Luna 9, in February 1966, made the first controlled landing and sent back the first pictures from the lunar surface. Its success proved the lunar surface could support a spacecraft. In the same year, Luna 10 became the first craft to orbit the Moon.

Luna 3 took the first photographs of the far side of the Moon.

Luna 3

ASTRONAUT TRAINING AND SELECTION

THE US SERIES OF MISSIONS TO SEND humans to the Moon was called Apollo. The astronauts chosen for the missions underwent months of training to prepare them for their journey. They prepared for the challenges of space, and trained for the work they had to do on each part of their journey. Hours were spent in mock-up spacecraft learning flying and landing procedures. They practised tasks such as eating in space, as well as emergency routines. They prepared their bodies for the different forces they would feel, from the increased gravity at launch, to the weightlessness of space, and the reduced gravity on the Moon's surface.

Weightlessness

A SPECIAL AIRCRAFT following a flight path called a parabolic loop can produce weightless conditions.

KC-135 plane at the top of its loop

7,000 m

6,000 m

5,250 m

Reduced gravity
As the plane flies on the downward part of its path, anyone inside feels weightless for about 25 seconds. Though gravity is still there, passengers cannot feel it because they are falling around the Earth.

FEELING WEIGHTLESS
Weightlessness can be achieved for only a short period of time during the flight of a specially adapted aircraft. Astronauts in their spacesuits made about 40 flights to practise moving while weightless.

The plane is padded to prevent injury.

Technicians secure themselves so that they can help the astronauts.

When the astronauts are weightless, they "fly" around inside the craft.

Astronauts appear to be upside down, but there is no up or down in the weightlessness of space.

To move forward, an astronaut needs to move backwards in space.

MOON WALKING
Astronauts prepared for getting around on the Moon by walking while they were supported by a sling and wires. The apparatus held an astronaut's body parallel to the ground and took 5/6ths of his weight to simulate the Moon's gravity.

UNDERWATER TRAINING
A giant water tank containing a mock-up of the lunar module helped astronauts prepare for the weaker gravitational pull on the Moon. They wore weights on their suits to give them buoyancy and practised getting into and out of the mock-up of the lunar module.

Increased gravity

WHEN ASTRONAUTS accelerate away from Earth and then decelerate on return to Earth, they feel increased gravity. The first experience is within seconds of liftoff. For a short time, the force felt is 3G, three times the usual pull of gravity.

Testing the human body
Before any human had flown into space, tests were carried out to see if the human body could cope with increased gravity. Once it was proved that it could, astronauts prepared for the greater gravitational forces of space flight.

Spinning around
A centrifuge machine helps to prepare astronauts for the increased forces they will feel when they travel into space. The astronaut (on the left above) is strapped into a seat and spun round and round to experience forces up to 8G.

A harness secured his body.

The head and facial features were pushed back.

The deceleration force was 22G.

1 In 1954, to test responses to sudden changes in force, Lieutenant Colonel John Stapp was sent hurtling down a track at Holloman Air Force Base, USA.

2 Stapp roared down the track for five seconds reaching speeds of over 970 kph (600 mph). The effect of the force of 12G can be seen on his face.

3 The seat jolted to a stop. Stapp's head lurched forward, he was blinded for a few seconds, and gained black eyes when blood surged to his face.

KEEPING COOL
The astronauts practised wearing their spacesuits and moving around on rough terrain. One important job of the suit was to keep the wearer's temperature constant. The astronaut on the right is wearing water-cooled underwear under his suit. On the left, the material of an oversuit is tested.

FACT file

● The first US astronauts were recruited in 1959. They were all male, under 40 years of age, and qualified jet pilots with 1,500 hours of flying experience.

● The typical Apollo astronaut was 1.8 m (5 ft 10 in) tall, weighed 72.5 kg (160 lb), and was 38.6 years old when he flew in space.

● Of the 29 Apollo astronauts, seven were left-handed, 22 were the first-born in their family, and 27 were married.

MAKING A LANDING
A vehicle nicknamed the "flying bedstead" was used to train for landing the lunar module. The craft would be flown by the commander of a mission. On one occasion, when Neil Armstrong was flying the bedstead, it began to tilt. He ejected safely before it crashed to the ground.

SAFE EXIT
In an emergency, an astronaut can eject from the training vehicle. He is catapulted high into the air and floats down by parachute.

The Lunar Landing Training Vehicle

Thrusters alter the position of the bedstead to prepare it for a smooth landing.

A computer on board eliminates 5/6ths of gravity to simulate lunar conditions.

Michael Collins
Neil Armstrong
Edwin Aldrin

The Apollo 11 crew
There were 29 astronauts who trained for the Apollo missions to the Moon. No one knew who would be the crew of three chosen to make the first landing. All the astronauts were capable of making that special flight. The crew was announced in January 1969. Neil Armstrong was to be the commander, and he would be accompanied to the lunar surface by Edwin "Buzz" Aldrin. Michael Collins would stay in orbit around the Moon.

PREPARING FOR THE MOON

ALL OVER THE US, PEOPLE WERE WORKING towards the first manned landing on the Moon. From 1961 onwards, thousands of workers, each concerned with a small part of the mission, prepared their contributions. As the astronauts trained and engineers designed and built the spacecraft, other teams prepared food, made clothes, devised tools for rock-collecting, and tested cameras to record the first steps on another world. Robotic craft were sent to photograph the lunar surface and find the right place for a lunar landing. Probes touched down to examine the surface on which astronauts would walk. Then the various parts of the complex journey were tried out by Apollo astronauts.

ON CAMERA
There were six television cameras inside the Ranger. They operated from when it first approached the Moon until it crash-landed on the surface.

Solar panels on either side provided the power for the cameras and for transmitting the pictures to Earth.

PHOTOGRAPHING THE MOON

A series of nine space probes called Ranger were designed to provide the first close-up views of the lunar surface. Only the final three in the series, launched between 1964 and 1965, were successful. They sent back more than 17,000 photographs showing detail that was invisible to telescopes on Earth.

Pineapple juice   Sugar cookies

Space food
The food for the Apollo astronauts had to be nutritious, ready to eat, easy to consume in weightless conditions, and neither bulky nor heavy. Some of the food was dehydrated; some was kept moist. Most food was in sealed pouches; the drinks pouches had a nozzle for sucking out the contents. The astronauts chose a menu for space from the 75 drinks and 100 food items available.

A camera with two lenses took photographs of the lunar surface.

RECORDED IMAGES
The information from the camera was recorded and radioed to Earth, where images were built up in strips.

CLOSE-UP VIEW
Lunar Orbiter 2 was 45.7 km (28.4 miles) above the Moon's surface when it recorded this view on 28 November 1966. Orbiter's photographs showed the mountains and plains of the lunar landscape.

CHOOSING A LANDING SITE

Almost the entire surface of the Moon was mapped by five Lunar Orbiter space probes starting in August 1966. The craft also provided images of selected areas that were then used to choose a landing site for the crewed missions. Orbiter developed its photographs on board and relayed the results back to Earth.

MAKING A LANDING

Seven Surveyor craft travelled to the Moon between June 1966 and January 1968. Their purpose was to make a soft-landing on the Moon using a retro-engine to slow their descent. On board were scientific instruments that tested the surface and a scoop that dug into the soil.

TESTING THE SURFACE
Surveyor photographed its own foot pad on the surface of the Moon, showing that a craft would not sink into the lunar soil.

A solar-powered television camera took pictures of the landscape in all directions.

Surveyor had shock-absorbing pads to help it to soft-land on the surface.

PRACTISING FOR THE MOON

Two Apollo missions carried men to the Moon before Apollo 11. The first crewed trip was made by Apollo 8, which orbited the Moon ten times. Apollo 10 also travelled around the Moon. Two of its crew, Thomas Stafford and Eugene Cernan (above), were within a few kilometres (miles) of the surface in the lunar module, while the third astronaut, John Young, orbited the Moon.

The Apollo spacesuit

CONDITIONS ON THE MOON'S SURFACE do not support human life. The Apollo spacesuit provided each astronaut with everything necessary to survive the Moon's environment.

Liquid-cooled garment worn under the suit

An outer helmet with gold visor

Link to oxygen and life-support system worn as a backpack

Suit made of strong fibres, metals, and plastics

A bubble helmet

Gloves with moulded fingertips

Outlet for transferring urine

A device for collecting urine

Lunar overshoe

Shoe with snap fastenings

Functions of the suit

The suit guarded the astronaut against micrometeoroids, tiny dust particles speeding through space. It controlled the astronaut's temperature by circulating cool water in an undergarment, and it protected the body against the lack of air pressure on the Moon.

TESTING AND BUILDING A ROCKET

IN MAY 1961, WHEN PRESIDENT KENNEDY PROMISED THAT the US would send a man to the Moon, there was no spacecraft capable of the task. So engineers and scientists set to work immediately to develop a suitable space vehicle. The Apollo craft was designed to carry the men to the Moon and bring them back to Earth again, and the Saturn V was created to launch them on their way. The various parts of Saturn V and Apollo were built and tested separately and then brought together at a specially constructed site at Cape Canaveral in Florida, USA. The area known as Complex 39 included a giant building called the Vehicle Assembly Building (VAB) where the rocket was put together.

Rocket scientist
Wernher von Braun was the director of the team that developed the Saturn V rocket for the Moon. In 1968, when the rocket for Apollo 11 was under construction, 26,500 men and women were working at Cape Canaveral, Florida, USA.

The Saturn V

MOST OF THE SATURN V rocket was filled with fuel. The Apollo 11 craft occupied a small part of the rocket.

Launch escape tower
Command module (*Columbia*)

Saturn V's cargo
The Apollo 11 takes up only the top end of Saturn V. Apollo 11 is made up of three parts, the command module *Columbia*, the service module, and the lunar module *Eagle*.

Service module
Lunar module (*Eagle*)

The crew entered the spacecraft through the white room, 122 m (400 ft) above the ground.

The instrument unit was used for control and communication between Saturn V and Apollo.

The third stage moved Apollo into Earth orbit and then pointed it towards the Moon.

The Vehicle Assembly Building

A huge crane lifted the Apollo craft into position.

Super Guppy
The "Super Guppy" carried spacecraft parts to the VAB. It was one of two specially adapted planes with enlarged upper decks. The whole front section of the planes opened for loading and unloading.

BUILDING THE PARTS

The Saturn V is made up of three stages, each with a different role to perform during the rocket's launch and short flight. These stages and the Apollo craft were constructed by different engineering firms at locations across the US. Once the parts were completed and tested they were brought to the VAB for assembly.

The tanks fed kerosene fuel and liquid oxygen to an F-1 engine, during tests in California, USA.

A ramp covered by a constant stream of water kept the flames down.

Once complete, the Saturn V was as tall as a 24-storey building. It was 111 m (363 ft) high and powerful enough to lift the 45-tonnes (50-ton) Apollo craft off the ground.

Each of the three rocket stages had engines, a fuel tank, and an oxygen tank needed to burn the fuel.

The second stage, and below it the first stage, lifted the rocket off the ground and into space.

The first Saturn V rocket had been launched in 1966; this was the sixth Saturn V rocket.

The launch site

The rocket left the VAB two months before liftoff. The Saturn V moved through the giant doors and into the open air to start its journey to the launch pad 39A, 5.6 km (3.5 miles) away, by a crawler. A new launch site for the missions had been built on 566,600 hectares (140,000 acres) of land.

Nine swing arms connected the launch tower to the various levels of the Apollo and Saturn V craft.

The crawler could raise or lower one of its corners to keep the rocket level.

The five engines of the first stage extended into the 14 m² (45 ft²) hole of the mobile launcher platform. At launch the engine's flames went into a flame trench.

CRAWLING ALONG

The crawler moved on eight tank-link tracks, each one 12.5 m (41 ft) long. It carried the Saturn V and its mobile launcher, which together weighed 6,000 tonnes (6,600 tons) at 1.6 kph (1 mph).

THE FINAL CHECKS

Inside the VAB, the parts were placed on top of each other and then checked and rechecked many times to see if the rocket worked when it was all together. The complete checklist filled more than 30,000 pages. Television cameras were also used to monitor what was happening. Once the final test sequence – a mock countdown that took the rocket to within 14 seconds of liftoff – was successfully completed, the craft was approved for launch.

The driver in the operator's cab was one of a 15-person crew who manoeuvred the crawler.

GAS GUZZLERS

The engines consumed 15 tonnes (16.5 tons) of fuel per second at launch.

MOST POWERFUL ENGINES

Each of the rocket's stages had engines. The most powerful were those built for the first stage, which had to lift the rocket and its Apollo cargo off the launch pad. The five F-1 engines would only burn for two and a half minutes but in that time they would generate 3,450,000 kg (7,600,000 lb) of thrust to lift the 2,630-tonne (2,900-ton) Saturn V. They were the most powerful engines ever built.

Blast Off!

ARMSTRONG, ALDRIN, AND COLLINS SAT CALMLY on top of the largest rocket in the world. Sealed inside the Saturn V, the astronauts carefully ran through their final checklist. The launch control countdown was nearly complete. Thirty seconds to liftoff and everything was fine; the astronauts reported feeling good. Their incredible journey to the Moon was about to begin.

"Three...two...
one...zero.
All engines running.
LIFTOFF!....
We have a liftoff,
32 minutes past the
hour. Liftoff on
Apollo 11....
Tower cleared."

Apollo 11 Launch Control
16 July 1969

In an emergency, the escape tower would carry the astronauts in the command module clear of the launch site.

The crew were located in the command module at the top of the rocket.

THE DAY OF LIFTOFF

THE CREW OF APOLLO 11 HAD AN EARLY CALL on 16 July 1969. They were awakened at 4:15 a.m. and after a brief medical examination they sat down for breakfast. Today's menu was special. It was steak, eggs, toast, orange juice, and coffee. It would be their last meal for a while. In four hours' time they would be sitting inside the Apollo command module (*Columbia*) at the top of the Saturn V rocket waiting to blast off to the Moon. The five-hour task of filling the rocket with fuel was almost complete. Now the three men, Neil Armstrong, commander, Edwin Aldrin, lunar module pilot, and Michael Collins, command module pilot, had to put on their spacesuits and travel to the launch pad.

Columbia was named after the Italian explorer Christopher Columbus.

REST DAY
On Tuesday 15 July, the day before the launch, the crew had a rest day. This gave them the chance to relax before the demanding work of the next ten days. In the evening, the astronauts dined with their stand-by crews and their trainer.

SUITING UP
5:30 a.m. When the men arrived in the suiting-up room, everything was ready. The lead suit technician Joe Schmitt had been checking their clothes for the past two hours. Armstrong packed a snack into his suit before he dressed.

WALKING OUT
6:26 a.m. The men walked out from the living quarters to the transfer van to be taken to the launch pad. They carried their life-support systems as they walked. Their suits and the van bore the mission badge, showing an American eagle landing on the Moon. The lunar module was named *Eagle*.

INTO THE ROCKET
6:52 a.m. The men left the surface of Earth when they stepped into the lift for the 32-second ride to the top of Saturn V. Waiting for them was the "close out" team. They helped the men into their seats, hooked up their suit hoses, and checked that *Columbia* was ready.

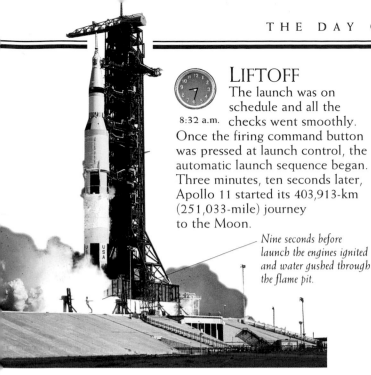

LIFTOFF

8:32 a.m. The launch was on schedule and all the checks went smoothly. Once the firing command button was pressed at launch control, the automatic launch sequence began. Three minutes, ten seconds later, Apollo 11 started its 403,913-km (251,033-mile) journey to the Moon.

Nine seconds before launch the engines ignited and water gushed through the flame pit.

Into space

THE SATURN V rocket carried Apollo 11 into space to start its journey to the Moon.

Liftoff for the Moon
The liftoff was perfect and everything went as expected. The first few seconds of flight were noisy and jerky, but they were followed by a smooth ride through Earth's atmosphere. Only 11 minutes after liftoff, Apollo orbited Earth at 29,000 kph (18,000 mph).

Nine minutes, 15 seconds after liftoff, Saturn V was in space. The third stage engine put the craft into Earth orbit.

Second stage jettisoned (cast off)

Launch escape tower jettisoned

Second stage engine ignited

Two minutes, 42 seconds after liftoff, the first stage was jettisoned.

The close out team worked in an area called "the White Room".

SEALED INSIDE *The arm swung back 43 minutes before launch.*

WAITING TO BOARD *Collins, and in front of him, Aldrin, waited as Armstrong climbed into Columbia.*

ONE MILLION SPECTATORS

The day was hot and sunny with thin cloud, the best weather for a launch. One million people travelled to Florida, USA, to watch the beginning of the Apollo 11 journey. Though they couldn't see the astronauts, the astronauts could see the crowds from the top of the launch tower.

ON THE SHORE *Crowds stood along the shore in Florida to watch the Saturn V rocket on the launch pad.*

FACT file

- Apollo began its journey not aimed at the Moon, but at where the Moon would be in three days' time.
- Five hours, 15 minutes, after launch, the astronauts ate their first meal in space: beef, potatoes, and grape juice.
- Fourteen hours after liftoff, the crew fastened covers over *Columbia's* windows and settled down to sleep.
- As the Apollo craft travelled, it rotated slowly, so that one side would not face the Sun constantly and overheat.

Heading for the Moon

THE APOLLO CRAFT separated from the final stage of the Saturn V rocket and prepared for the Moon.

Apollo docking
The Apollo craft and the third stage of the Saturn V rocket orbited Earth, and then moved onto a path for the Moon. After turning and docking manoeuvres, the astronauts discarded the Saturn V rocket.

The combined command and service module separated from the rocket 3 hours and 15 minutes after liftoff.

The module turned around. Panels protecting the lunar module were discarded.

The command module docked with the lunar module and moved away from the third stage of the rocket.

MISSION CONTROL

ARMSTRONG, ALDRIN, AND COLLINS were on their way to the Moon. Though there were only three men in the craft, a team of people back on Earth felt that they were travelling with them. Every movement made by the craft or men was followed inside the mission operations control room, in Houston, Texas, USA. The engineers and technicians in this room kept in touch with the astronauts through sea-, air-, and land-based tracking stations. They made sure everything went according to plan and were ready for any emergency.

Flight director
The officer in charge of the control room and its work was the flight director. If any problems arose, the flight director was the person to make the final decision, after consulting the team members. Gene Kranz (above) was flight director for the landing.

Capsule communicator
The link between the control room and Apollo 11 was the capsule communicator, usually called "capcom". He handled all communication between Earth and the spacecraft. Capcom for the landing on the Moon was Charles Duke (above).

The front row of consoles was called "the trench".

Screens displayed the progress of the mission.

Experiments officer

Capcom

Flight director

Operations and procedures officer

Control room team

EACH CONTROL ROOM TEAM was made up of smaller teams led by a controller or officer. They sat and worked together in the control room.

 Flight dynamics officer
This officer is responsible for planning spacecraft manoeuvres and monitoring the path taken by Apollo 11.

 Experiments officer
When the astronauts are on the surface, this officer relays information between them and scientists on Earth.

 Flight surgeon
The flight surgeon monitors the health of the crew during the course of the flight.

 Flight activities officer
This officer plans the crew's tasks, and makes sure they follow their checklists and schedules during the flight.

 Network controller
This controller coordinates the worldwide network of communication links.

 Retrofire officer
If something goes badly wrong on a mission, the retrofire officer advises on when to return home.

CONTROL ROOM

Four teams took turns working around the clock at mission control. Once a team was in position, the doors were locked so that they couldn't be disturbed. Each member of the team monitored a part of the mission. This might mean studying the route of Apollo 11, guiding its descent to the Moon, or checking the health of the crew. The teams sat at computer consoles displaying up-to-date information on their area of responsibility.

GLOBAL LINK

Three large antennas based in Australia, Spain, and California, USA, were the core of the tracking system. The antenna at Honeysuckle Creek, near Canberra, Australia, was 26 m (85 ft) in diameter.

antennas flew ... land or

On track for the Moon

APOLLO 11'S MISSION started in Florida, USA. The Saturn V rocket lifted the craft into orbit around Earth and then on course for the Moon.

Mid-course correction

Apollo 11 orbited the Moon

Columbia docked with Eagle.

Into Moon orbit
After orbiting Earth, they moved on course for the Moon, and Saturn V's job was over. When Apollo 11 and its crew reached the Moon, they went into orbit around it and prepared for *Eagle* to separate and land on the Moon.

MC
Aldr
after
he f
expe
he r
mos

The tracking ship Vanguard *was positioned in the Atlantic Ocean.*

KEEPING TRACK

A network of ground, ship, and air tracking stations called the Manned Spaceflight Network (MSFN) allowed mission control to know where Apollo was at any time. It also relayed messages between capcom and the astronauts.

COMMUNICATING

Four tracking ships not only helped to locate Apollo 11 but also worked as part of the communication system. They relayed information from the craft and the men.

Flight dynamics officer

Network controller

Steve Bales, guidance officer

Gene Kranz, flight director

R
Ar
US
in
Pr
pr
ha

SPECIAL GUESTS
Off-duty officers, astronauts, family, and invited guests watched from a glassed gallery.

DECISION TO LAND

As Armstrong and Aldrin moved closer to the Moon, an alarm sounded. In the control room a flashing light let the ground team know that the *Eagle's* computer had too many jobs to do at once. Flight director Gene Kranz consulted guidance officer Steve Bales. Could the landing go ahead? The message "We're go" was passed to Armstrong.

HOMEWARD BOUND

THE APOLLO 11 astronauts heard the engines roar and knew they were on their way home. The engines burned (fired) for a short time to push the craft out of the Moon's orbit and on its way back to Earth. *Eagle*, which had lifted Armstrong and Aldrin from the lunar surface, had been jettisoned. Just two parts of the Apollo craft, the command and service modules, would make the journey back. The men received congratulations from the ground crew and settled down for a well-earned sleep. They rested for 10 hours. A major part of their mission was now over, but the hazardous re-entry into Earth's atmosphere, followed by the splashdown in the Pacific Ocean, still lay ahead.

RADIO SILENCE
Radio links with the ground ceased for about 15 minutes as they travelled through the upper atmosphere.

Friction, caused by the craft rushing through the air, heated the outside of the capsule.

HEAT SHIELD
The walls of the capsule were built like a multi-layered sandwich. The outer heat shield was designed to burn off.

HEATING UP
Inside the craft, the temperature remained a constant 27°C (80°F). Temperatures on the base of the craft reached 2,760°C (5,000°F).

Back to Earth

THE ASTRONAUTS STARTED their journey home in the combined command and service modules.

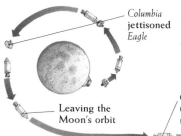

Columbia jettisoned Eagle

Leaving the Moon's orbit

RETURN TRIP
The journey home began when Apollo 11 left Moon orbit on 22 July 1969. As the module re-entered Earth's atmosphere it was travelling at almost 40,300 kph (25,000 mph).

Correction to *Columbia's* course to slow it down

Separation of command and service modules

Re-entering Earth's atmosphere

Preparing for Earth's atmosphere
The service module was jettisoned before it reached Earth's atmosphere. *Columbia* was travelling nose first until thrusters were used to turn it round so that the blunt end was pointing towards Earth. The Earth's atmosphere slowed the craft.

THROUGH EARTH'S ATMOSPHERE
As they headed towards Earth, Armstrong, Aldrin, and Collins showed the world on a live television broadcast the Moon rocks they had collected. Close to Earth, they jettisoned the service module. *Columbia* with its cargo of men and rocks would be the only part of Apollo 11 to return to Earth. The craft sped through the atmosphere, burning up on the outside. Inside, Armstrong used small thrusters to control the direction of the craft.

SLOWING DOWN
At 6,000 m (20,000 ft) above the ground, and with Columbia travelling at 525 kph (325 mph), the parachute landing system started.

The cone tip of Columbia was cast off and two parachutes were used to help slow down the craft.

PARACHUTE FALL
The location for splashdown was chosen before the craft entered the atmosphere. There were two tropical storms near the recovery area that had to be avoided. The module was directed towards good weather where the visibility was 16 km (10 miles). Once through the upper atmosphere, the module's parachutes slowed the craft in its last stage of descent.

INTO THE OCEAN
At 3,000 m (10,000 ft) the three main parachutes opened slowing the module to 32 kph (20 mph). Columbia splashed down exactly 195 hours and 18 minutes after leaving Earth.

The recovery ship Hornet took the astronauts and their module to Hawaii, from where they flew to Houston, Texas, USA.

The blunt side was designed to slow down the craft on its return to Earth.

The Mobile Quarantine Facility
Richard Nixon, President of the USA, was on board *Hornet* waiting to welcome the three astronauts home. After a shower and shave, they appeared at the window and joined in prayers of thanksgiving for their safe return. The astronauts stayed in quarantine for two weeks in the Lunar Receiving Laboratory, Houston, USA, where they were examined by doctors.

The helicopter Recovery 1 flew the astronauts the short distance from the dinghy to the lower deck of Hornet.

SPLASHDOWN
Columbia splashed down into the Pacific Ocean. It floated upside down, until Collins activated three flotation bags stowed in the module's nose. Within five minutes, the craft was upright. Two rescue teams in their dinghies and frogmen in the water moved towards the module. The rescue ship *Hornet* was close by, ready to take the astronauts home.

BACK ON EARTH
The men had their first experience for several days of walking in Earth's gravity, as they moved from the helicopter to the MQF.

The Mobile Quarantine Facility (MQF) was home to the astronauts for three and a half days.

The frogmen placed a flotation collar around the module to stop it from sinking.

A frogman cleaned the hatch of the module with disinfectant to kill any Moon germs.

The recovery dinghies were disinfected and then sunk.

CLIMBING OUT
A frogman opened the door of the module and passed special overalls to the three men. The astronauts put these on to protect others from the Moon dust on their clothes. Once in the dinghy, Armstrong, Collins, and Aldrin were hoisted aboard the helicopter.

Welcome home
Once they were out of quarantine, the three astronauts could relax and celebrate with their families and people around the world. Vast numbers of people turned out to see them in the 23 countries they visited in a 38-day tour. In New York City, USA, they were welcomed with a ticker-tape (paper ribbon) parade.

Later Missions

WITHIN MONTHS OF THE FIRST MEN RETURNING SAFELY to Earth, a second crew was heading towards the Moon and others were preparing to go, too. In all, 12 men landed on the Moon – two more astronauts had to abandon their plans and return disappointed. Since 1972, exploration has been restricted to robotic craft, but today a new generation is preparing to return to the Moon.

Apollo missions 12 to 17 carried men to the Moon. Each astronaut wore a badge on his spacesuit displaying the names of the crew members.

Apollo 12

Apollo 13

Apollo 14

An electric car, the Lunar Rover, transported astronauts and equipment across the Moon's surface.

Apollo 15

Apollo 16

Apollo 17

The Lunar Rover

EXPLORING THE MOON

FIVE MORE APOLLO MISSIONS CARRIED astronauts to the Moon. These later missions could concentrate on making a scientific investigation of the lunar landscape. The astronauts worked in four-hour shifts, collecting samples and setting up experiments. Although the men only stayed for a few days at a time, the experiments operated for several years. The first crews carried their tools or pulled them along on a handcart. But in the later missions they used a Rover for getting about. This unique lunar car gave them the freedom to travel away from their landing site. By the time the last mission left the Moon, its different types of landscape: mare, lowlands, highlands, and craters had all been explored.

Laser reflector experiment
The astronauts set up experiments such as this laser ranging retro reflector. Its upper mirrored surface reflected a laser beam back to Earth to provide information on the Moon's orbit.

Seismometer equipment
Other experiments were part of a package. These consisted of a number of experiments linked to a central transmitter. This seismometer collected data on moonquakes.

Rock collecting

THE ASTRONAUTS' SPACESUITS restricted their movements. The gloves were thick and clumsy, and the astronauts were unable to bend in their suits. Special tools were designed to make it possible to collect rocks without bending. These tools had to be transported from site to site along with boxes of rock samples. Though they weren't heavy in the Moon's gravity, they were bulky to carry around.

A tool rack fitted into the frame of the rickshaw.

The air-pumped tyres became stuck in deep Moon dust and the rickshaw had to be carried.

Collecting box

Brush

Scoop

Metal fingers grasped the rock.

Tongs

Collecting box and tools
The astronauts had a range of tools to collect different types of samples such as chunks of rock and fine dust. Scoops, tongs, and bore tubes were used. The astronauts briefly described the sample and the site it came from, put it in a bag and then in a storage box.

The rickshaw
The Apollo 14 astronauts had a Modularised Equipment Transporter for carrying their tools, cameras, and samples. This handcart, usually called a "rickshaw", was pulled along by the astronauts and allowed them to collect a greater number of samples.

The Rover

THE ROVER WAS CARRIED to the Moon underneath the lunar module. It was lowered for use.

Unfolding the Rover
The Rover was complete but folded for the journey. Once on the Moon, an astronaut pulled two cords to lower it. Each end of the vehicle unfolded and the wheels moved out into position.

THE FINAL MISSION
The last manned mission to the Moon, Apollo 17, began on 7 December 1972. It was the first manned launch at night. Two of the crew, Eugene Cernan and Harrison Schmitt, spent the longest time on the lunar surface – 22 hours. Schmitt, a geologist, was the only scientist to land on the Moon.

A plaque like this one, was fixed to the descent stage of Challenger, which was left behind on the Moon.

The plaque marked the end of human exploration of the Moon.

A MESSAGE
The Apollo 17 lunar module, named Challenger, landed near the edge of the Mare Serenitatis. When the astronauts blasted off on 14 December 1972, they left behind a plaque.

Antenna   Television camera

Hand control for driving

Antenna for communication

The wheels were made of wire mesh and each contained its own motor.

COMMUNICATION
The astronauts could talk to each other as they worked, through a communication antenna in their backpack.

Tools were fitted in a rack at the back of the Rover. Rock samples were placed in front of the rack and under the seats.

MOON ROVING
A Lunar Roving Vehicle, usually called the "Rover", was used on Apollos 15, 16, and 17. It was a lightweight car powered by two batteries and had a top speed of 18.6 kph (11 mph). The astronauts used it to travel up to 9.6 km (6 miles) from their landing site. They could not travel any farther because if the Rover broke down, it would be too far to walk back.

The Rover was built mainly from aluminium, a lightweight metal that helped to reduce the weight of the Apollo's cargo.

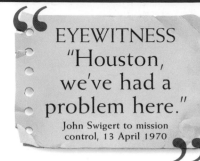

EYEWITNESS
"Houston, we've had a problem here."
John Swigert to mission control, 13 April 1970

DISASTER STRIKES!

JAMES LOVELL, JOHN SWIGERT, AND FRED Haise were approaching the Moon on the Apollo 13 mission. They were looking forward to exploring its surface. The men had just completed a television broadcast when they were interrupted by a sharp bang. A warning light flashed on, and the Apollo craft shuddered. Something was wrong. The men discovered that there had been an explosion in the service module that provided the crew with vital power and life-support systems. Things couldn't have been worse. They were 330,000 km (205,000 miles) from Earth heading for the Moon without the power to turn round.

DESPERATE MEASURES
Apollo 13 travelled around the Moon. It used the lunar module's engine to put the craft on a course back towards Earth.

LIFE-SUPPORT SYSTEM
The lunar module was designed to support two men for two days on the Moon. It was now needed to support three men for four days.

There was an explosion in the service module.

Oxygen tank number 1 was damaged, and its contents escaped into space.

A course correction aimed Apollo 13 at Earth.

The service module

A whole panel of the service module was blown off.

The lunar module

The astronauts moved into the lunar module, which had its own supply of oxygen, water, and power.

The command module

Oxygen tank number 2 blew up.

FIRE AND DEBRIS
Pieces of insulating foil were blown out into space. The flames stopped when all the oxygen had escaped.

Oxygen tank
The number 2 oxygen tank had overheated and exploded. Its temperature should have been controlled, but the switches had welded shut. The temperature of the tank should not have been higher than 27°C (80°F) but it soared to 538°C (1,000°F).

EXPLOSION!
The crew reported the explosion to mission control. The warning lights told them they had lost their main source of electricity. They knew this meant the planned landing on the Moon would be abandoned, but disappointment quickly turned to thoughts of survival. Every effort from the astronauts and mission control was needed to get the men home.

BRING THEM HOME
Four teams at mission control, the black, gold, white, and maroon teams, worked in shifts around the clock to find the best way to bring Apollo 13 back home. They decided to use the lunar module's engines to bring the astronauts back.

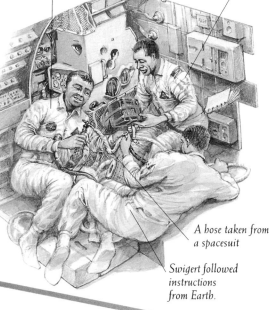

MORE PROBLEMS

Haise told mission control that the lunar module had enough oxygen and power to make the journey home, if they turned off everything that was not essential. But the lunar module was filling with the carbon dioxide that the crew were breathing out. Ground teams worked to build something to take the carbon dioxide out of the air.

The ground team used only the items that could be found on Apollo 13, such as cardboard, tape, and plastic bags.

Haise watched the work.

Command module's air-cleaning equipment was adapted for the lunar module.

COLD AND DAMP

Conditions inside the lunar module were grim. The temperature dropped to 3°C (38°F). Water condensed on the walls, and the windows were covered with frost. The men found it hard to sleep. The food they ate was very cold and altogether they lost 14 kg (31.5 lb) in weight.

SAVING THEIR LIVES

After one and a half days, and before the carbon dioxide level became dangerous, the ground crew built a piece of equipment to clean the carbon dioxide from the air in the lunar module. Inside the command module, Lovell and Swigert were led step-by-step through the process to build the same piece of equipment. One hour later, they had finished, and another problem was solved.

A hose taken from a spacesuit

Swigert followed instructions from Earth.

Relief and disappointment
The astronauts were picked up from the Pacific Ocean by the recovery ship *Iwo Jima*. They were all hungry, tired, dehydrated, and cold. In the final hours before recovery they had used stay-awake pills to keep them alert. The flight was a disappointment for Lovell; he had now travelled to the Moon twice without landing on it.

Apollo 13 made a course adjustment and headed for a lunar landing.

GETTING CLOSER
The lunar module that acted as a lifeboat for the three astronauts, had done its job, now that they were close to Earth.

Apollo 13 started its journey from Earth on 11 April 1970.

The crew had their first look at the damage and photographed it.

THE FINAL HOUR
The astronauts moved from the lunar module to the command module for the journey through Earth's atmosphere.

A SAFE RETURN
The command module and its crew of three astronauts splashed down on 17 April. The mission was described as a successful failure because of the men's safe return.

NO MORE USE
About four hours before splashdown, the crew jettisoned the useless service module.

THE FINAL STAGE

The three astronauts travelled towards Earth in the lunar module and then moved into the command module for the final stage of the journey. They turned on its equipment; it was cold and wet but operated as normal. The wrecked service module and the lunar module were jettisoned now that their work was over.

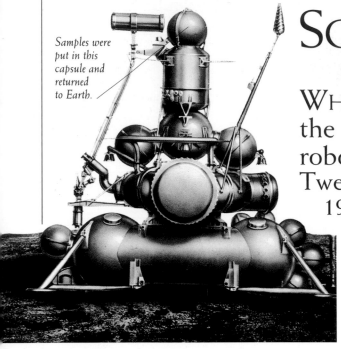

Samples were put in this capsule and returned to Earth.

SCIENTIFIC INVESTIGATIONS

WHILE THE US WAS BUSY SENDING MEN TO the Moon, Soviet rockets were launching robotic probes to explore the lunar surface. Twenty-four Luna missions were sent between 1959 and 1976. Three brought back rock to Earth and two carried mobile scientific laboratories to work on the Moon's surface. In the eighteen years following the final Luna mission, neither crewed nor robotic craft were sent to the Moon. Scientists continued to work on information and samples that had already been collected. Much of the Apollo rock was studied at the specially built Lunar Sample Building in Houston, USA.

ROCK SAMPLES

Luna 16 was the first robotic probe to bring back rock from the Moon. The probe made a controlled landing on the Moon in September 1970. Luna 16's drill collected a sample from 35 cm (14 in) below the surface. The drill was in the lower part of the probe. The upper part of the probe had its own engine and fuel, and returned the sample to Earth.

Luna 20 returned to Earth during a snowstorm on 25 February 1972.

FURTHER SAMPLES

Luna 20 brought the second sample back to Earth in February 1972. The sample of soil from beneath the surface of the Moon was well protected on its journey. The outside of the returning capsule screened the rock from the high temperatures of the Earth's upper atmosphere. A parachute slowed the probe's fall and a radio signal indicated its location.

X-ray telescope

Aerial

Scientific instruments sealed inside the instrument bay

Radiator to keep Lunokhod 1 cool

Equipment to turn the aerial to point towards Earth for receiving and sending information.

Television camera

Soil analysis equipment

ROBOT EXPLORER

Lunokhod 1 was the first of two robotic craft to move about the lunar surface and work at different sites. It landed in the Mare Imbrium in November 1970. During the next ten months it moved over 10.45 km (6.5 miles) of the lunar surface. Operators on Earth controlled its movements. It returned over 20,000 pictures to Earth and tested the soil at 500 points. A second, upgraded Lunokhod arrived on the Moon to start work in 1973. It worked for less than five months but travelled farther, 37 km (23 miles).

Moon rocks

THE APOLLO ASTRONAUTS collected 2,000 samples of rock, pebbles, sand, dust, and core material. The samples were studied around the world.

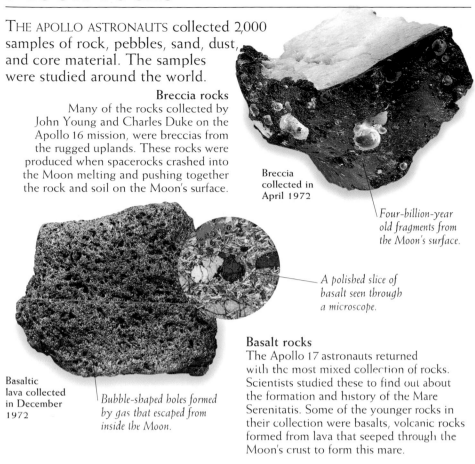

Breccia rocks
Many of the rocks collected by John Young and Charles Duke on the Apollo 16 mission, were breccias from the rugged uplands. These rocks were produced when spacerocks crashed into the Moon melting and pushing together the rock and soil on the Moon's surface.

Breccia collected in April 1972

Four-billion-year old fragments from the Moon's surface.

A polished slice of basalt seen through a microscope.

Basaltic lava collected in December 1972

Bubble-shaped holes formed by gas that escaped from inside the Moon.

Basalt rocks
The Apollo 17 astronauts returned with the most mixed collection of rocks. Scientists studied these to find out about the formation and history of the Mare Serenitatis. Some of the younger rocks in their collection were basalts, volcanic rocks formed from lava that seeped through the Moon's crust to form this mare.

Clementine's survey
When the space probe Clementine moved into orbit around the Moon in February 1994, it was the first US craft to investigate the Moon since Apollo 17 more than 20 years earlier. Clementine made a photographic survey of 99 per cent of the Moon's surface, including the polar regions, during the following three months.

Lunar Prospector
Instruments aboard the Prospector probe started work on 12 January 1998, as the craft orbited 100 km (62 miles) above the lunar surface. Data from the instruments suggested that water in the form of ice is mixed with surface soil in the polar regions, particularly around the North Pole. If the findings are correct, parts of the Moon may not be dry and lifeless after all.

The lid was kept closed at night to prevent heat loss.

Camera to take vertical views

Lunokhod 1 was 7.2 m (23.6 ft) long.

Solar cells on the inside of the lid converted sunlight into electrical power.

Camera to take horizontal views

The eight wheels had titanium bars to grip the lunar surface.

Lunokhod 1

OUR FUTURE ON THE MOON

MANY OF THE MEN AND women who worked on the Moon missions, such as Apollo 11, are now grandparents. Their work is being continued by a new generation of space technicians in countries around the world. New space workers are developing what we've learned about the Moon, space travel, and how humans cope in space, and are ready to put new technologies into practice. They, like those before them, are fascinated by the Moon and want to walk on its surface. Their aim is to set up a base where they can live and work for several months at a time.

Spacecraft will transport workers and visitors to and from Earth or around the Moon.

SPACECRAFT TRAVEL
Everything needed for life, including oxygen, water, and food, will be carried to the Moon to set up the first base. Specially designed crewless craft can be used time after time to transport these items as well as building materials.

If any part of the telescope stopped working it could be repaired in the lunar workshop.

The telescope has "feet" and can "walk" to a new site.

NO WEATHER
A telescope wouldn't need a dome to protect it from the weather like Earth telescopes — there is no weather on the Moon.

Mining the Moon's resources
Studies of the Moon's rock and soil show that it can be used to make concrete to build a lunar base. It also contains the elements aluminium, and iron, which could be mined and used to make building materials; silicon could also be extracted and used to insulate lunar homes and make solar panels.

MOON OBSERVATORY
The Moon would be a very convenient place to set up telescopes for looking farther into space. Because it has no atmosphere, there are no clouds to spoil the view. Telescopes would be operated by remote control by astronomers on the Moon or on Earth.

> "There is no reason why we could not return to the Moon – but this time to stay."
> US Office of Exploration

LUNAR POWER
The Sun shines continuously on the Moon during the day. Its energy can be collected in solar cells and converted to electricity.

KEEPING IN TOUCH
Moon workers wanting to stay in touch with friends and relatives back on Earth, would communicate using dish antennas.

Vehicles with wide wheels or tank-link tracks would be used for short journeys.

Holiday destination
Many people would love a trip to the Moon, and their chance may come soon. This hotel has been designed for the first lunar tourists. It has 5,000 rooms, its own beach and sea, as well as a medical centre, church, and school.

FOOD FARMS
Regular food shipments from Earth would cost too much, and supplies would not last long. Food would be grown on the Moon in enclosed, climate-controlled buildings.

PARKS
Food-growing areas would double as parks where Moon dwellers could take a walk without needing to wear a spacesuit.

New equipment

EQUIPMENT FOR OUR return to the Moon is already being made. An important development is a safe and comfortable spacesuit. The new design will enable men and women to walk, bend, and turn easily.

Gloved hand
The spacesuit glove protects the hand inside but allows it to feel. The checklist, written on paper in the days of Apollo, is now an electronic memo.

HOME AWAY
Workers spending months on the Moon would need some earthly comforts. Off-duty time could be spent watching television programmes from Earth or by keeping fit in the air-sealed sports hall.

MOON DATA

THE MOON IS AN ENORMOUS ball of rock that shines in our sky by reflected sunlight. Our present knowledge of it is based on what we see through telescopes on Earth and in space, and on information collected by the Apollo missions and scores of other spacecraft that have investigated the Moon. We know not only what the Moon is like today, but also how it was formed and what it was like in the past.

THE NEAR SIDE

The same side of the Moon, called its near side, always faces Earth. Dark and light areas on the surface are easily visible from Earth. Early observers mistook the dark regions as seas and called them "maria", the Latin word for seas.

The dark, low-lying maria (singular mare) are huge craters filled with lava.

Mare Tranquillitatis is one of the largest maria and was the landing site for Apollo 11.

Copernicus is a young, bright crater.

MARE IMBRIUM
MARE SERENITATIS
MARE CRISIUM
OCEANUS PROCELLARUM
MARE TRANQUILLITATIS
MARE FECUNDITATIS
Copernicus
Alphonsus
Tycho

LANDING SITES

17 Luna missions
17, 21

11 Apollo missions
11, 12, 14, 15, 16, 17

NEAR SIDE

The Moon is covered with craters, bowl-shaped hollows in its surface that formed when space rocks crashed into it.

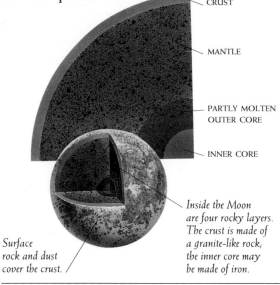

CRUST
MANTLE
PARTLY MOLTEN OUTER CORE
INNER CORE

Inside the Moon are four rocky layers. The crust is made of a granite-like rock; the inner core may be made of iron.

Surface rock and dust cover the crust.

The Moon's structure

The Moon is a sphere of rock about a quarter of the size of Earth. It is a dry world without atmosphere, life, or geological activity. It is Earth's only Moon and accompanies our planet as it orbits the Sun.

Facts and Figures

DIAMETER	3,476 KM (2,158 MILES)
AVERAGE DISTANCE FROM EARTH	384,400 KM (239,000 MILES)
ORBIT AROUND EARTH	27.3 DAYS
ORBITAL SPEED	1.02 KM/SECOND (0.6 MILES/SECOND)
ONE SPIN ON ITS AXIS	27.3 DAYS
CYCLE OF PHASES	29.5 DAYS
TEMPERATURE	-155°C TO 105°C (-247°F TO 221°F)
GRAVITY (EARTH = 1)	0.16
MASS (EARTH = 1)	0.012

THE MOON'S PAST

Most scientists believe the Moon was formed from Earth about 4,500 million years ago. The young Moon's surface became covered in craters and lava.

Formation of the Moon
A rock about the size of Mars crashed into the young Earth, splashing molten rock into orbit around it. The material joined together to form a big, molten Moon.

As the Moon cooled, its rock started to solidify and a crust formed on its surface. Craters appeared when space rocks crashed into the crust.

About 3,000 million years ago, molten rock started to ooze through the crust and created maria, seas of lava on part of the Moon's surface.

Today's Moon looks like the Moon of about 2,000 million years ago. There have been no major changes, just some new craters.

4,500 MILLION YEARS AGO

3,800 MILLION YEARS AGO

2,800 MILLION YEARS AGO

TODAY

THE FAR SIDE

The Moon's far side is invisible from Earth. Only the Apollo astronauts who flew to the Moon have seen it. The rest of us can see it in photographs taken by spacecraft. Like the near side, it is covered with craters, but has fewer, smaller maria.

Mare Moscoviense is one of the few maria on the far side. Less lava broke through on this side, because the crust is much thicker.

This side would be a good location for a telescope to study space.

MARE MOSCOVIENSE

Gagarin

Tsiolkovsky

Apollo

MARE ORIENTALE

MARE AUSTRALE

The dark lava-filled crater Tsiolkovsky has a mountain range in the centre.

Mare Orientale on the edge of the far side is a 900-km (560-mile) wide crater surrounded by high mountains. The crater floor is flooded with lava.

FAR SIDE

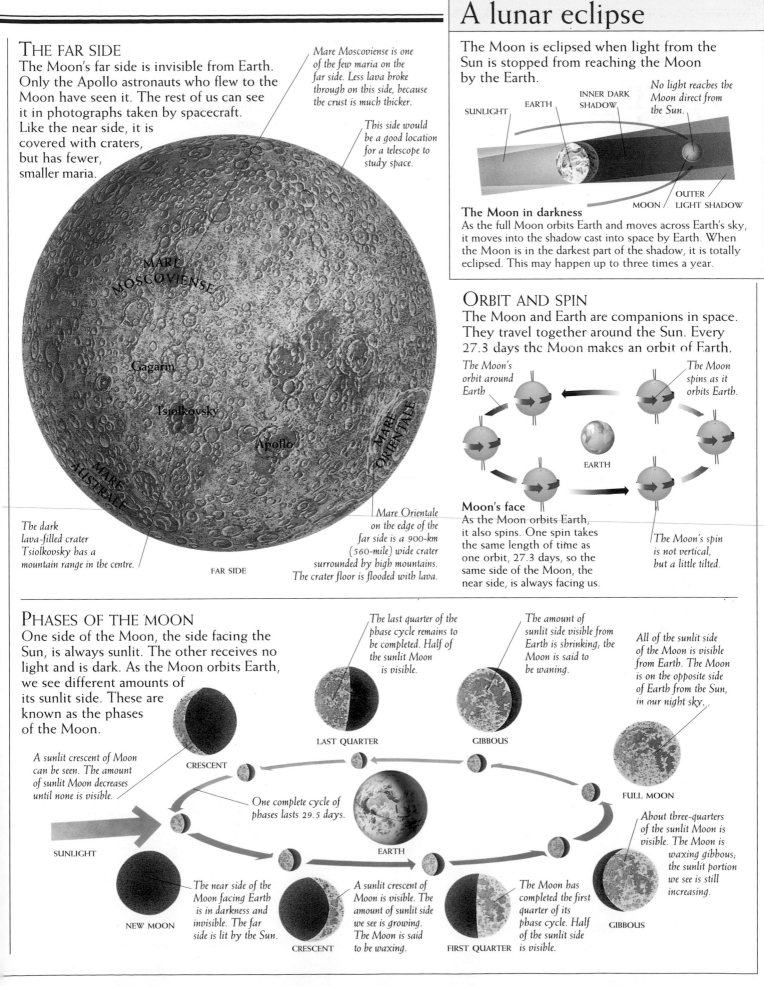

A lunar eclipse

The Moon is eclipsed when light from the Sun is stopped from reaching the Moon by the Earth.

SUNLIGHT • EARTH • INNER DARK SHADOW • *No light reaches the Moon direct from the Sun.* • MOON • OUTER LIGHT SHADOW

The Moon in darkness
As the full Moon orbits Earth and moves across Earth's sky, it moves into the shadow cast into space by Earth. When the Moon is in the darkest part of the shadow, it is totally eclipsed. This may happen up to three times a year.

ORBIT AND SPIN

The Moon and Earth are companions in space. They travel together around the Sun. Every 27.3 days the Moon makes an orbit of Earth.

The Moon's orbit around Earth

The Moon spins as it orbits Earth.

EARTH

Moon's face
As the Moon orbits Earth, it also spins. One spin takes the same length of time as one orbit, 27.3 days, so the same side of the Moon, the near side, is always facing us.

The Moon's spin is not vertical, but a little tilted.

PHASES OF THE MOON

One side of the Moon, the side facing the Sun, is always sunlit. The other receives no light and is dark. As the Moon orbits Earth, we see different amounts of its sunlit side. These are known as the phases of the Moon.

The last quarter of the phase cycle remains to be completed. Half of the sunlit Moon is visible.

The amount of sunlit side visible from Earth is shrinking; the Moon is said to be waning.

All of the sunlit side of the Moon is visible from Earth. The Moon is on the opposite side of Earth from the Sun, in our night sky.

LAST QUARTER

GIBBOUS

A sunlit crescent of Moon can be seen. The amount of sunlit Moon decreases until none is visible.

CRESCENT

One complete cycle of phases lasts 29.5 days.

FULL MOON

SUNLIGHT

EARTH

About three-quarters of the sunlit Moon is visible. The Moon is waxing gibbous; the sunlit portion we see is still increasing.

The near side of the Moon facing Earth is in darkness and invisible. The far side is lit by the Sun.

NEW MOON

A sunlit crescent of Moon is visible. The amount of sunlit side we see is growing. The Moon is said to be waxing.

CRESCENT

The Moon has completed the first quarter of its phase cycle. Half of the sunlit side is visible.

FIRST QUARTER

GIBBOUS

MOON MISSIONS

LISTED BELOW ARE THE MOST successful missions to the Moon; including space missions that prepared the way for the first manned landing.

Sputnik 1
The first artificial satellite to orbit Earth. Launched by the Soviet Union on 4 October 1957. Successfully marked the start of the Space Age.

Sputnik 2
The first living creature to travel into space, Laika, a mongrel dog. Launched by the Soviet Union from Baikonur Cosmodrome, on 3 November 1957.

Luna 1
The first craft to leave Earth's gravity. The Soviet probe left Earth on 2 January 1959, and flew within 5,630 km (3,500 miles) of the Moon.

PIONEER 4

Pioneer 4
The first US probe to the Moon, launched two months after Luna 1. Three previous attempts had failed when the rockets couldn't achieve the necessary speed.

LUNA MISSIONS

Luna 2
The first craft to land on the Moon and the first to land on another world outside our own. Crashed into the Moon on 13 September 1959.

Luna 3
Luna 3 was launched on the second anniversary of Sputnik 1. It flew round the Moon. On 7 October 1959, it radioed back to Earth the first pictures of the far side of the Moon.

Vostok 1
Soviet cosmonaut Yuri Gagarin travelled aboard Vostok 1 and became the first human in space on 12 April 1961. He completed one orbit of Earth and landed safely, separate from his craft.

Mercury 3
Astronaut Alan Shepard was the first American in space. His flight in the Freedom 7 capsule lasted 15 minutes 22 seconds before splashdown on 5 May 1961.

Vostok 2
Gherman Titov was the second person in orbit and the first to spend more than 24 hours in space. The Soviet cosmonaut started his journey on 6 August 1961.

Mercury 6
John Glenn was the first US astronaut to fly in orbit around Earth. He was launched from Cape Canaveral on 20 February 1962. He made three orbits in *Friendship 7*.

Vostok 6
The first woman in space was Soviet cosmonaut Valentina Tereshkova. Vostok 6 was launched on 16 June 1963, and spent 71 hours in space, orbiting Earth 38 times.

Cameras provided the first close-up photographs of the Moon.

RANGER 7

Ranger 7
The seventh craft in the first US space programme to explore the Moon. Ranger 7 crashed into the Moon on 31 July 1964.

Voskhod 1
First three-man capsule into space, launched on 12 October 1964. Crew flew without spacesuits – no room for the Soviet cosmonauts to wear them. First live television transmission from space.

Ranger 8
Launched on 17 February 1965. Crash-landed in the Mare Tranquillitatis, and transmitted over 7,000 photographs before impact on the Moon's surface.

Voskhod 2
Soviet cosmonaut Alexei Leonov made the first spacewalk on 18 March 1965. He was secured by a tether to his Voskhod 2 capsule.

Ranger 9
In March 1965, the last in the Ranger series transmitted nearly 6,000 photographs of the lunar surface before it crash-landing in the Alphonsus Crater.

Gemini 3
The first US two-man crew in space, launched on 23 March 1965. Virgil Grissom and John Young were also the first American astronauts to manoeuvre a craft in space.

Gemini 4
Ed White was the first US astronaut to walk in space in June 1965. He remained linked to his Gemini capsule by a tether during his 22-minute spacewalk.

Zond 3
A Soviet probe, launched on 18 July 1965, was destined for Mars; however, it flew past the Moon and sent back photographs of the Moon's far side.

Geminis 6 and 7
First US space rendezvous (meeting in space) in December 1965. The two craft, each with two astronauts on board, met in orbit. Also the first time that there were four astronauts in space at the same time.

Luna 9
The first soft-landing on the Moon. Luna 9 sent the first television pictures from the lunar surface on 3 February 1966.

Gemini 8
The first space docking. Americans David Scott and Neil Armstrong flew into space on 16 March 1966, to dock with an unmanned Agena rocket.

Luna 10
The first spacecraft to orbit the Moon. It achieved orbit on 3 April 1966, and started a study of the lunar surface.

SURVEYOR MISSIONS

Surveyor 1
The first US probe to soft-land on the Moon. On 2 June 1966, it landed in the Oceanus Procellarum, tested the soil, and sent back over 11,000 photographs.

Lunar Orbiter 1
The first of five US probes to orbit and map the Moon. Orbiter 1 started work in August 1966 looking for lunar landing sites. On 29 October 1966, Orbiter 1 was deliberately crashed into the surface to make room for Orbiter 2.

Lunar Orbiter 2
Orbiter 2 continued the work of Orbiter 1 from November 1966. It located 13 possible landing sites before crashing to the lunar surface to make room for Orbiter 3.

MEN ON THE MOON
The only humans to travel to the Moon were 26 US Apollo astronauts, all men. Of these, 12 walked on its surface, spending 80 hours exploring six different sites. The first to land was Neil Armstrong on 20 July 1969; the last was Eugene Cernan on 14 December 1972.

1969		1970

APOLLO 11
NEIL ARMSTRONG
EDWIN ALDRIN

APOLLO 12
CHARLES CONRAD
ALAN BEAN

Luna 13
A Soviet probe launched on 21 December 1966, that soft-landed on the Moon. It transmitted pictures of the surface and used an arm-digger to examine the composition of the lunar surface.

Lunar Orbiter 3
The third US Orbiter probe to orbit and photograph the Moon to help identify Apollo landing sites. It was launched on 4 February 1967.

Surveyor 3
A US probe soft-landed on the Moon in April 1967. It tested the lunar soil and transmitted over 6,000 photographs of the surface. It remained in operation until early May 1967.

A camera with two lenses took photographs of the lunar surface.

LUNAR ORBITER

Lunar Orbiter 4
A US probe launched on 4 May 1967, that orbited and mapped the Moon. It took the first photographs of the Moon's south pole. After transmitting its pictures to Earth it crashed to the lunar surface to avoid Lunar Orbiter 5.

Lunar Orbiter 5
The last of the Orbiter series of probes designed to orbit and map the Moon. It transmitted photographs to Earth before crashing into the lunar surface on 31 January 1968.

Surveyor 5
A US probe soft-landed in the Mare Tranquillitatis on 10 September 1967. It transmitted over 18,000 photographs and tested the lunar soil.

Surveyor 6
Launched on 7 November 1967, Surveyor 6 made a soft-landing on the Moon. It tested for a future liftoff from the Moon, rising 3 m (10 ft) above the ground.

Surveyor 7
The last Surveyor probe to the Moon. It landed near the crater Tycho in January 1968, tested the soil, and took photographs.

Zond 5
A Soviet spacecraft sent on 14 September 1968, to test equipment for a manned mission to the Moon. On board were turtles, worms, and flies. This was the first flight to circle the Moon and return to Earth.

Zond 6
The second Soviet craft launched to test equipment for a manned mission to the Moon. Sent on 10 November 1968, it circled the Moon and returned to Earth.

ZOND

Apollo 8
First crewed flight of the Saturn V rocket on 21 December 1968 – the first manned craft to leave Earth's gravity. William Anders, James Lovell, and Frank Borman, were the first to orbit the Moon.

Apollo 9
First manned flight of spacecraft parts to be used in a Moon landing. In a ten-day trip in March 1969, the crew docked with the lunar module in Earth orbit.

APOLLO 10

Apollo 10
A dress rehearsal for the lunar landing. American astronauts Tom Stafford and Eugene Cernan flew the lunar module close to the lunar surface on 22 May 1969.

Luna 15
Soviet probe Luna 15 was launched for the Moon on 13 July 1969. It failed in its attempt to land a rover on the Moon and to return with a soil sample to Earth.

Apollo 11
The first humans, US astronauts Neil Armstrong and Edwin Aldrin, walked on the Moon on 20 July 1969. Returned to Earth with Michael Collins.

Apollo 12
Second manned landing on the Moon. Landed on the Oceanus Procellarum on 19 November 1969. Walked to Surveyor 3, which had landed in 1967.

Apollo 13
An oxygen tank on Apollo 13 exploded in April 1970. The craft didn't land on the Moon but returned to Earth safely.

Luna 16
First robotic probe to collect Moon soil and return it to Earth. Landed at Mare Fecunditatis on 20 September 1970.

Luna 17
First wheeled vehicle on the Moon. Lunokhod 1 explored Mare Imbrium from 17 November 1970. Tested the soil and sent back television pictures.

Apollo 14
Third manned landing on the Moon. Touched down on 5 February 1971, in the Fra Mauro hills. Used the rickshaw to carry tools, and collected a large number of rocks.

Apollo 15
Fourth manned landing on the Moon and the first to use the Lunar Rover. Touched down on 30 July 1971, at Hadley Rille. Collected rock.

Luna 20
Second Soviet mission to collect rock samples from the Moon. Brought back soil from Mare Crisium in February 1972.

Apollo 16
Fifth manned landing on the Moon on 20 April 1972. Landed in the lunar highlands and used the second Lunar Rover to collect many rocks.

Apollo 17
Sixth and last manned mission to the Moon, landed on 11 December 1972, in the Littrow Valley. The Lunar Rover covered a greater area and collected a large number of rocks.

Luna 21
Carried the rover Lunokhod 2 to the surface of the Moon. Lunokhod 2 explored the surface for almost five months, until 3 June 1973.

Luna 23
Soviet probe launched to the Moon on 28 October 1974. Made a soft-landing and returned soil samples to Earth.

LUNA

Luna 24
The last Soviet probe to bring back Moon soil to Earth. Samples were taken by drilling below the lunar surface in August 1976.

Hiten
Probe launched to the Moon by Japan on 24 January 1990. Hiten carried a second probe, Hagoromo, making Japan only the third nation to put a craft into orbit around the Moon.

CLEMENTINE

Clementine
In February 1994, this US probe moved into orbit around the Moon. It started a programme of mapping and investigating the lunar surface.

Lunar Prospector
US spacecraft Lunar Prospector went to the Moon in January 1998. Instruments investigating the Moon's surface detected signs of water ice near the north pole.

LUNAR PROSPECTOR

1971   1972

APOLLO 14
ALAN SHEPARD
EDGAR MITCHELL

APOLLO 15
DAVID SCOTT
JAMES IRWIN

APOLLO 16
JOHN YOUNG
CHARLES DUKE

APOLLO 17
EUGENE CERNAN
HARRISON SCHMITT

Index

Acknowledgments

The publisher would like to thank: Anna Martin for design assistance, Chris Bernstein for the index, Robert Graham for research, and Lee Thompson for picture research.

Dorling Kindersley would like to thank the following institutions: Moscow Museum, NASA Johnson Space Centre and Headquarters Washington, Polytechnic Museum Moscow, Science Museum London, US Space and Rocket Centre, Alabama.

The publisher would like to thank the following for their kind permission to reproduce their photographs:

a=above; c=centre, b=below; l=left; r=right; t=top;

BFI/Association des Amis de George Méliès Voyage to the Moon Spadem 6–7 tr; **UPI/Corbis** 26 cla, 26 tl, 31 cr; **Corbis/Bettmann** 24 cb, N.A.S.A 14 br; **UPI/Corbis Bettmann** 24 cl, 25 cr; **John Frost Historical Newspapers/Evening Standard** 11 crb: **Genesis Space Photo Library/NASA** 16 clb, 46 clb, 20 cl, 24 clb, 46 clb; **Image Bank:** Isy-Schwart 6–7 cla; **Peter**

Inston/Inston Design International 43 tr; **Courtesy of N.A.S.A.:** 8 crb, 12–13, 14 cl, 15 clb, 15 cb, 17 cla, 17 crb, 17 bl, 18 crb, 18–19 tc, 18 c, 19 tc, 19 clb, 20 br, 20 tr, 22-23, 25 tl, 27 tl, 27 cra, 30 ca, 33 bl, 33 crb, 33 tr, 34–35, 35 tc, 35 tl, 35 tr, 35 cla, 35 ca, 35 cra, 36 bl, 36 tl, 36 la, 37 cra, 37 tr, 38 rb, 38 rb, 38 lb, 39 tl, 39 tr, 41 ca, 41 crb, 41 cr, 42 clb, 43 br, 46 c, 47 cl, 47 ca, 47 br; **Natural History Museum, London** 41 cra, 41 tl; **Novosti (London):** 9 cb, 10 tl, 11 tr, 14 tl, 15 tl, 17 tc, 40 tl, 40 lb, 47 clb, 47 clb, 47 cr;

Oxford Scientific Films: Stan Osilinski 6-7; **Science & Society Picture Library:** 18 bl, 18 bc; **Novosti/Science Photo Library:** 9 cr; **Small Space Photos:** 30 tr; **Sovfoto/Eastfoto** 46 cla, 46 cla, 47 tr; **Carole Stott:** 46 cr; **Topham Picturepoint:** 17 tr; **TRH Pictures** 16 bc.

Jacket:
Image Bank: Isy-Schwart back cra; **NASA:** front inside flap, front c, front cla, front cla, front bl, back inside flap, **Novosti/Science Photo Library:** back crb; **US Space & Rocket Museum Alabama:** back bc.